First Facts

Materials

Glass

by Mary Firestone

Capstone press

Mankato, Minnesota

First Facts is published by Capstone Press
151 Good Counsel Drive, P.O. Box 669, Mankato, Minnesota 56002
www.capstonepress.com

Copyright © 2005 by Capstone Press. All rights reserved.
No part of this publication may be reproduced in whole or in part, or stored in a retrieval system, or transmitted in any form or by any means, electronic, mechanical, photocopying, recording, or otherwise, without written permission of the publisher.
For information regarding permission, write to Capstone Press,
151 Good Counsel Drive, P.O. Box 669, Dept. R, Mankato, Minnesota 56002.
Printed in the United States of America

Library of Congress Cataloging-in-Publication Data
Firestone, Mary.
Glass / by Mary Firestone.
p. cm.—(First facts. Materials)
Includes bibliographical references and index.
ISBN 0-7368-2650-5 (hardcover)
1. Glass—Juvenile literature. 2. Glass manufacture—Juvenile literature. I. Title. II. Series.
TP857.3.F47 2005
666'.1—dc22   2004000370

Summary: Discusses features of glass including how it is manufactured and made into useful products we use everyday.

Editorial Credits
Heather Adamson, editor; Jennifer Bergstrom, series designer; Molly Nei, book designer; Scott Thoms, photo researcher; Eric Kudalis, product planning editor

Photo Credits
Capstone Press/Gary Sundermeyer, front cover, 5, 6–7, 12–13
Corbis/James L. Amos, 9, 19; Michael Prince, 14; Sygma/Pitchal Frederic, 10
Folio Inc./Regis Lefebure, 16–17
Houserstock/Dave G. Houser, 11
MoonCave Crystals, 20
PhotoDisc Inc, back cover, 1, 15

First Facts thanks the staff of the Corning Museum of Glass, Corning, New York, for consulting on this book.

1 2 3 4 5 6   09 08 07 06 05 04

Table of Contents

Glass 4

What Is Glass? 7

Materials for Making Glass 8

Melting and Molding 10

Crystal 12

Flat and Curved 14

Colored Glass 17

Recycling Glass 18

Amazing but True! 20
Hands on: Glassblower's Skills 21
Glossary 22
Read More 23
Internet Sites 23
Index 24

Glass

Alice pours breakfast cereal into a bowl. She sips orange juice from a glass and checks her watch. The sun shines through the window. Glass is all around us.

What Is Glass?

Glass is a hard substance people make from **silica**. Silica is crushed into sand to make glass. Limestone and **soda ash** are often mixed with silica. They help silica melt better. People use glass every day.

Fun Fact!
Machines can make as many as 2,300 glass lightbulbs in one minute.

Materials for Making Glass

The materials in glass are found in the ground. Workers collect silica near rivers and oceans. Soda ash can be mined in salt **quarries**. Limestone is also dug from quarries. Workers break apart the soda ash and limestone with machines.

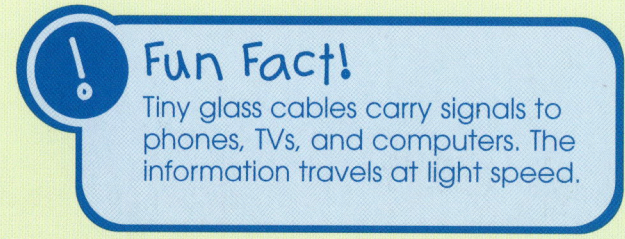

Fun Fact!
Tiny glass cables carry signals to phones, TVs, and computers. The information travels at light speed.

Melting and Molding

Factory workers melt sand, soda ash, and limestone in big ovens. Machines press **molten** glass into **molds**. When it cools, the glass becomes hard.

Some artists blow glass. They place **gobs** of molten glass at the end of long tubes. They blow in the tubes to shape the glass. Machines can also blow hollow items, such as bottles.

Crystal

Crystal is a type of glass that has extra sparkle in the light. Metal is added to glass to make crystal. Drinking glasses, lamps, and candy dishes are often made of crystal.

Fun Fact!
Dip your finger in water with vinegar and rub the edge of a crystal glass. It will make a high-pitched sound.

Flat and Curved

Flat glass is easy to see through. It is used to make aquariums, windows, doors, and mirrors.

14

Curved glass is used to make lenses. Lenses can make things look bigger or smaller. Many cameras, binoculars, and microscopes use curved glass lenses.

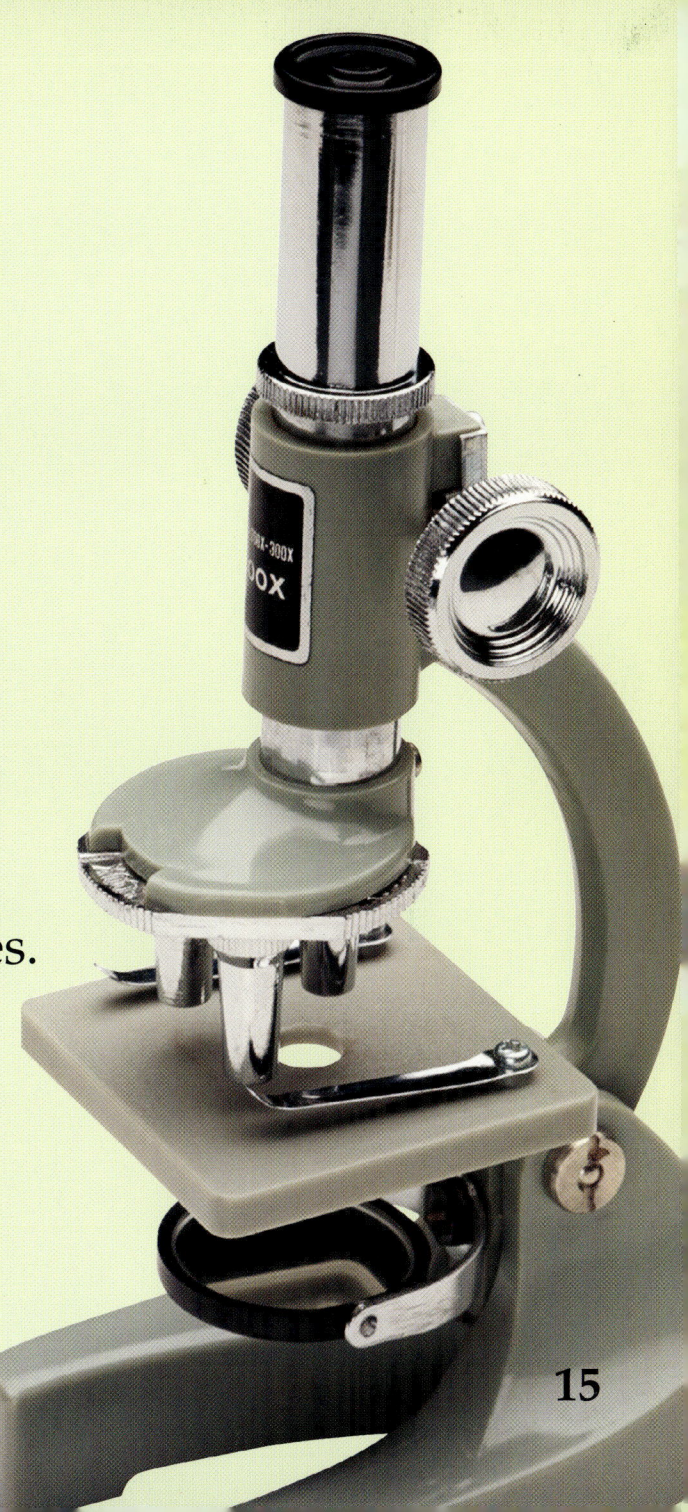

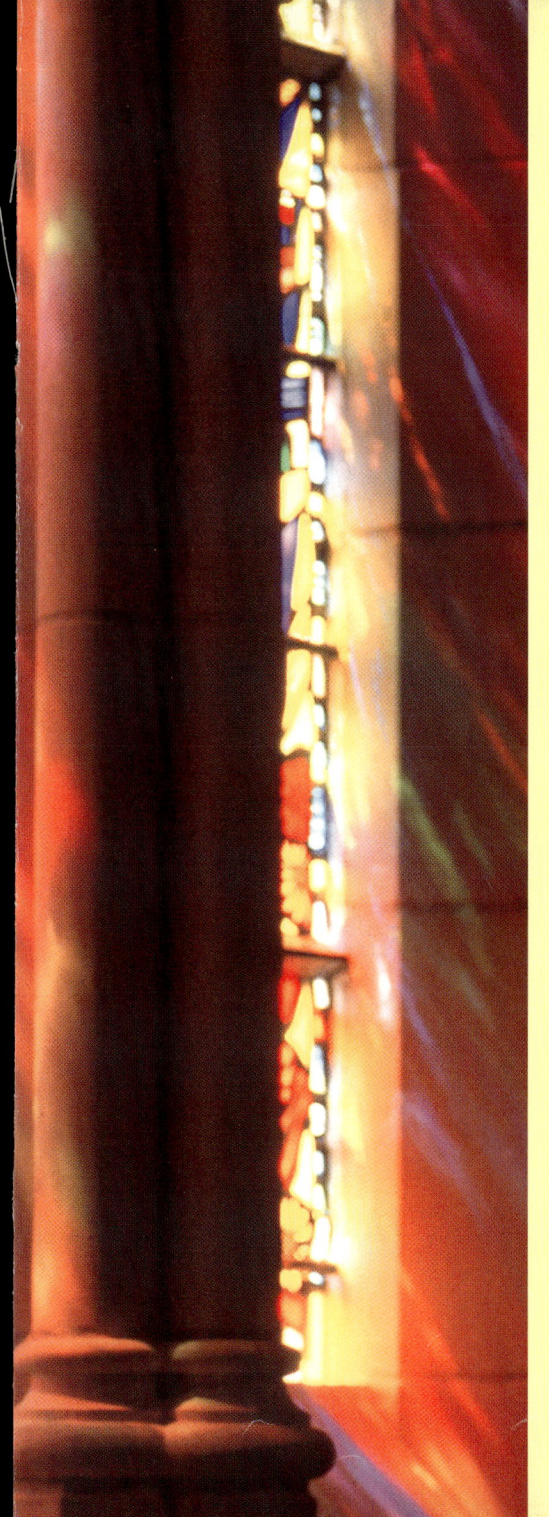

Colored Glass

Glass can be made in different colors. Most often color is added to molten glass. Stained glass is made by baking the color onto the glass after it hardens.

Artists use small pieces of colored glass to make pictures. These pictures are called **mosaics**.

Recycling Glass

Glass can be recycled. Glass bottles and jars are broken into small pieces by machines. The pieces are called **cullet**. Cullet is melted down to make new glass bottles and jars.

Fun Fact! Marbles are made from recycled glass.

Amazing but True!

Nature makes its own glass. When lightning strikes sand, lightning heats the sand to nearly 3,000 degrees Fahrenheit (1,650 degrees Celsius). The sand melts into crusty glass tubes. This glass is called fulgurite.

Hands On: Glassblower's Skills

Glass blowers must be able to twist and balance molten glass on the edge of their tubes as they blow. Try this activity to test your glassblowing skills.

What You Need

small bowl of honey
medium bowl of ice
chopstick

What You Do

1. Place the small bowl of honey in the medium bowl filled with ice. Let the honey get cold.
2. Touch the surface of the honey with the tip of the chopstick. Turn the stick slowly on the surface. See if you can form a small ball on the end of the stick. Do not let the honey ball drop off of the stick.

When you stop turning the stick, the honey starts to slide off the stick. Glassblowers must keep their tubes spinning to form glass into an even shape.

Glossary

cullet (KUHL-it)—pieces of broken glass

gob (GOB)—a small blob of melted glass

mold (MOHLD)—a shaped container

molten (MOHLT-uhn)—melted by heat into a liquid; molten glass can be poured into molds.

mosaic (moh-ZAY-ik)—pictures or patterns made from small, colored shapes; pieces of colored glass can be used to make mosaics.

quarry (KWOR-ee)—a place where people use machines to dig minerals and rock from the ground

silica (SIL-uh-kah)—a type of stone mined from the ground

soda ash (SOH-duh ASH)—a common salt called sodium carbonate

Read More

Oxlade, Chris. *How We Use Glass.* Using Materials. Chicago: Raintree, 2004.

Parker, Steve. *Glass.* Materials. Milwaukee: Gareth Stevens, 2002.

Internet Sites

FactHound offers a safe, fun way to find Internet sites related to this book. All of the sites on FactHound have been researched by our staff.

Here's how:
1. Visit *www.facthound.com*
2. Type in this special code **0736826505** for age-appropriate sites. Or enter a search word related to this book for a more general search.
3. Click on the **Fetch It** button.

FactHound will fetch the best sites for you!

Index

binoculars, 15
bottles, 11, 18

cameras, 15
crystal, 12
cullet, 18

fulgurite, 20

glassblowing, 11
gobs, 11

jars, 18

lenses, 15
lightning, 20
limestone, 7, 8, 10

machines, 8, 10, 11, 18
microscopes, 15
mining, 8
molds, 10
mosaics, 17

quarries, 8

recycling, 18

sand, 7, 10, 20
silica, 7, 8
soda ash, 7, 8, 10
stained glass, 17

windows, 4, 14